Python for AI:

: A Beginner's Guide to Grasping AI Concepts and
Developing Basic Machine Learning and Data
Science Applications with Python"

.

Matthew D.Passmore

Table Of Content

Chapter 8: Data Preparation and Exploration

8.1. Loading and cleaning data for machine learning tasks

8.2. Visualizing and analyzing data

Chapter 9: Machine Learning Algorithms

9.1. Introduction to common algorithms (linear regression, decision trees)

9.2. Training and evaluating models

Part 4: Building Basic AI Applications with Python

Chapter 10: Building a Simple Recommender System

10.1. Using collaborative filtering to recommend items

Chapter 11: Creating a Chatbot with Natural Language Processing (NLP)

11.1. Introduction to NLP concepts

Part 1: Introduction

Chapter 1
What is Artificial Intelligence (AI)?

Artificial intelligence (AI) is a broad field of computer science that deals with creating intelligent machines capable of mimicking human cognitive functions. Here's a breakdown of the key aspects:

Core Concepts:

Machine intelligence: AI focuses on developing machines that can reason, learn, solve problems, and make decisions like humans.

Automation: AI automates tasks that are typically performed by humans, such as image recognition, speech recognition, and data analysis.

Learning: AI systems can learn from data and improve their performance over time. This can be achieved through various techniques like machine learning and deep learning.

Types of AI:

There are different categories of AI based on their capabilities:

Narrow AI (ANI): Also known as weak AI, these are the most common type. They are trained for specific tasks and excel in them, like playing chess or recommending products.

Artificial General Intelligence (AGI): This hypothetical type of AI would possess human-level intelligence and be able to perform any intellectual task a human can. AGI currently doesn't exist.

Artificial Superintelligence (ASI): This even more theoretical concept refers to an AI surpassing human intelligence in all aspects.

Overall, AI is a rapidly evolving field with the potential to revolutionize many aspects of our lives.

1.1. Understanding the core concepts of AI

Artificial intelligence (AI) has transformed from science fiction to a prominent force shaping our world. But what exactly is it, and how does it achieve intelligent behavior? Here, we'll explore the fundamental concepts that underpin AI:

1. Machine Intelligence:

At its core, AI aspires to create machines that exhibit human-like intelligence. This encompasses several key capabilities:

Learning: The ability to acquire knowledge and skills from data, experience, or instruction. AI systems can learn from vast amounts of data to improve their performance on tasks.

Reasoning: The ability to use logic and available information to draw conclusions and make decisions. AI systems can analyze complex situations and choose optimal actions.

Problem-solving: The ability to identify problems, devise solutions, and implement them effectively.
AI can tackle intricate challenges by exploring various options and selecting the most promising ones.

2. Automation:

A hallmark of AI is its ability to automate tasks traditionally requiring human intervention. This automation can take several forms:

Perception: AI systems can perceive their environment through sensors like cameras and microphones. They can then interpret visual data (images, videos) or auditory data (speech) to understand the world around them.

Decision-making: Based on their perception and processing of information, AI systems can make informed decisions. This could involve taking actions in a simulated environment or controlling robots in the real world.

Action: Some AI systems are equipped to perform actions in the physical world. Robots guided by AI can manipulate objects, navigate complex terrains, or even perform surgery with high precision.

3. Learning Techniques:

AI systems wouldn't be nearly as impressive without their ability to learn. Here are two prominent approaches:

Machine Learning: This involves training AI models on massive datasets. The models identify patterns and relationships within the data, enabling them to make predictions or classifications on new, unseen data.

Deep Learning: A subfield of machine learning inspired by the structure and function of the human brain. Deep learning models, also known as neural networks, are composed of interconnected layers that process information progressively, mimicking how the brain learns.

By combining these core concepts, AI systems are constantly evolving and pushing the boundaries of what machines can achieve.

1.2. Different types of AI (Machine Learning, Deep Learning, etc.)

Artificial intelligence (AI) isn't a monolithic concept. It encompasses a diverse range of approaches, each with its own strengths and limitations. Let's delve into some of the key categories:

Machine Learning (ML): This is a powerful subfield of AI where algorithms learn from data without explicit programming. Here's the breakdown:

Training: ML models are trained on massive datasets, allowing them to identify patterns and relationships within the data.

Predictions: Once trained, the models can make predictions on new, unseen data. For instance, an

ML model trained on email data can predict spam with high accuracy.

Applications: Machine learning has a wide range of applications, from facial recognition in smartphones to spam filtering in email to product recommendations on e-commerce platforms.

Deep Learning (DL): A subset of machine learning inspired by the human brain. Here's what makes it unique:

Artificial Neural Networks: Deep learning utilizes artificial neural networks, complex algorithms with interconnected layers that mimic the structure and function of the brain.

Learning Hierarchy: Information is processed through these layers, allowing the network to learn complex features from data.

Applications: Deep learning excels at tasks requiring pattern recognition, such as image classification (identifying objects in pictures) or natural language processing (understanding and generating human language).

Narrow AI (ANI): Also known as weak AI, this is the most prevalent type of AI today. Here are its defining characteristics:

Specialization: ANIs are trained to perform specific tasks exceptionally well.

Limited Scope: They lack the general intelligence of humans and cannot adapt to significantly different situations outside their training domain.

Examples: Examples include chess-playing programs, image recognition software in self-driving cars, or chatbots providing customer service.

Artificial General Intelligence (AGI): This hypothetical type of AI would possess human-level intelligence, capable of performing any intellectual task a human can.

General Intelligence: AGI is still theoretical and doesn't currently exist. It would understand and learn any intellectual concept a human can.

Challenges: Achieving true AGI requires significant breakthroughs in areas like artificial consciousness and understanding the human brain.

Artificial Superintelligence (ASI): This even more theoretical concept refers to an AI surpassing human intelligence in all aspects.

Superintelligence: ASI is far beyond the foreseeable future. It would potentially have capabilities beyond human comprehension.

By understanding these different types of AI, we gain a deeper appreciation for the vast potential and ongoing development in this exciting field.

Chapter 2

Why Use Python for AI?

Python has become the go-to programming language for artificial intelligence (AI) development, and for good reason. Here's a closer look at the factors contributing to its dominance in this rapidly evolving field:

Readability and Simplicity: Python's syntax is known for its clarity and resemblance to natural language. This makes it easier to learn, write, and understand code, even for beginners. This is crucial in AI projects, where complex algorithms and data manipulation are involved.

Extensive Libraries and Frameworks: Python boasts a rich ecosystem of libraries and frameworks specifically designed for AI and machine learning (ML). These pre-built tools provide a wealth of functionalities, saving developers time and effort when building AI applications. Here are some popular examples:

NumPy: Provides powerful tools for numerical computations, essential for working with large datasets in AI.

Pandas: Offers data analysis and manipulation functionalities, streamlining data preparation for AI models.

TensorFlow: A popular deep learning framework enabling developers to build and train complex neural networks.

Scikit-learn: Provides a comprehensive collection of machine learning algorithms for various tasks like classification, regression, and clustering.

Strong Community Support: Python has a vast and active developer community. This translates to readily available online resources, tutorials, and forums. If you encounter problems or have questions, you're likely to find solutions and support from fellow Python programmers and AI enthusiasts.

Versatility and Scalability: Python's versatility allows it to be used for various stages of the AI development process, from data pre-processing to model training and deployment. Additionally, Python code can scale well for complex projects involving massive datasets and computationally intensive tasks.

Platform Independence: Python code can run on different operating systems (Windows, macOS, Linux) without modifications. This makes collaboration and deployment of AI projects across various platforms seamless.

In summary, Python's readability, extensive libraries, strong community support, versatility, and platform independence make it an ideal choice for anyone venturing into the world of AI development. Whether you're a beginner or a seasoned programmer, Python offers a powerful and user-friendly foundation for building intelligent applications.

2.1. Advantages of Python for AI development (readability, libraries, community)

Python has become the undisputed champion for artificial intelligence (AI) development. Its dominance can be attributed to several key advantages, particularly its readability, extensive libraries, and vibrant community support.

Readability for Crystal-Clear Code:

Python's syntax is renowned for its clarity and resemblance to plain English. This makes it much easier to learn, write, and understand code compared to languages with complex syntax. This is a game-changer in AI, where complex algorithms and data manipulation are the norm. Clear code translates to fewer errors, faster development cycles, and easier collaboration within AI teams.

A Treasure Trove of Libraries:

Python offers a rich ecosystem of libraries and frameworks specifically designed for AI and machine learning (ML). These pre-built tools function as building blocks, providing a vast array of functionalities that save developers significant time and effort when constructing AI applications. Popular examples include:

NumPy: The foundation for numerical computing, essential for handling large datasets in AI.

Pandas: Streamlines data preparation for AI models by offering data analysis and manipulation functionalities.

TensorFlow: A popular deep learning framework that empowers developers to build and train complex neural networks, a cornerstone of deep learning.

Scikit-learn: Provides a comprehensive collection of machine learning algorithms for various tasks, including classification, regression, and clustering. With these powerful libraries at their disposal, developers can focus on the core aspects of their AI projects, like model design and innovation.

A Community Where No One Gets Left Behind:

Python boasts a massive and active developer community. This translates to a wealth of readily available online resources, tutorials, forums, and even communities specifically dedicated to AI development with Python. If you encounter a hurdle or have a question, you're likely to find solutions and support from fellow Python programmers and AI enthusiasts. This fosters a collaborative and supportive environment, making it easier for beginners to enter the field and for experienced developers to stay up-to-date with the latest advancements in AI.

In conclusion, Python's readability, extensive libraries, and strong community support create a perfect trifecta for AI development. Whether you're a budding AI developer or a seasoned programmer, Python offers a powerful and user-friendly foundation to build intelligent applications and contribute to the ever-evolving field of artificial intelligence.

.

Chapter 3

Setting Up Your Python Environment

Before diving into the fascinating world of artificial intelligence (AI) development with Python, you'll need to establish a well-equipped development environment. Here's a roadmap to get you started:

Installing Python:

The first step is to download and install Python itself. Head over to https://www.python.org/downloads/ and choose the latest stable version compatible with your operating system (Windows, macOS, or Linux). The installation process is typically straightforward and includes clear instructions on the website.

Verifying Installation:

Once the installation is complete, open a terminal or command prompt (depending on your operating system) and type python --version (or python3 --version on some systems). This command should display the installed Python version, confirming successful installation.

Package Manager: pip

Python uses a package manager called pip to install additional libraries and frameworks. To verify pip is installed, type pip --version in your terminal. If not installed, refer to the official Python documentation for instructions on installing pip.

Installing Essential Libraries:

Now it's time to install the essential libraries you'll need for AI development. Here are some core ones to get you started:

NumPy: pip install numpy (numerical computing)

Pandas: pip install pandas (data analysis and manipulation)

Matplotlib: pip install matplotlib (data visualization)

Scikit-learn: pip install scikit-learn (machine learning algorithms)

You can install additional libraries as needed based on your specific AI projects.

Choosing a Development Environment (Optional):

While you can work with Python from the command line, using a dedicated development environment (IDE) can significantly enhance your experience. These IDEs offer features like code completion, debugging tools, and integration with popular version control systems (like Git) for managing your code. Some popular options for AI development with Python include:

Jupyter Notebook: A web-based interactive environment ideal for prototyping and experimentation.

PyCharm: A powerful IDE with extensive features specifically designed for Python development.
Visual Studio Code: A versatile code editor with various extensions to support Python development effectively.

As you progress, you might explore more advanced libraries and delve deeper into specific AI techniques. But with these foundational steps, you're well on your way to becoming a Python-wielding AI developer!

3.1. Installing Python and essential libraries (NumPy, Pandas, etc.)

Artificial intelligence (AI) is an exciting field, and Python is a powerful tool to bring your AI ideas to life. Here's a step-by-step guide to installing Python and the essential libraries you'll need:

1. Download and Install Python:

Head over to the official Python downloads page: https://www.python.org/downloads/
Choose the latest stable version compatible with your operating system (Windows, macOS, or Linux). Download the appropriate installer and follow the on-screen instructions. The installation process is typically straightforward.

2. Verify Python Installation:

Once the installation is complete, open a terminal or command prompt (depending on your operating system).

Type python --version (or python3 --version on some systems) and press enter.

This command should display the installed Python version, confirming successful installation.

3. Install the Package Manager pip (if not already installed):

Python uses pip to install additional libraries and frameworks.

To verify pip is installed, type pip --version in your terminal.

If pip is not installed, refer to the official Python documentation for instructions on installing it for your specific operating system.

4. Install Essential Libraries for AI Development:

Now you're ready to install the libraries that will be your companions on your AI journey. Here are some core ones to get you started:

NumPy (numerical computing): Run the command pip install numpy in your terminal.

Pandas (data analysis and manipulation): Use pip install pandas to install it.

Matplotlib (data visualization): Install it with pip install matplotlib.

Scikit-learn (machine learning algorithms): Run pip install scikit-learn for installation.

Additional Tips:

You can install other libraries as needed based on your specific AI projects. There are many powerful libraries available in the Python ecosystem.

Consider using a virtual environment to manage different project dependencies effectively.

Congratulations! You now have Python and essential libraries installed, ready to embark on your exploration of artificial intelligence.

Remember, this is just the first step. As you delve deeper, you'll encounter more specialized libraries and exciting AI techniques. But with this foundation, you're well on your way to becoming a proficient Python programmer equipped for AI development!

3.2. Introduction to Jupyter Notebooks or other development environments

Now that you're armed with Python and essential libraries, it's time to choose your development environment – your AI playground! Here, we'll explore Jupyter Notebooks, a popular option, and introduce you to other possibilities:

1. Jupyter Notebook: A User-Friendly Playground

Jupyter Notebook is a web-based interactive development environment specifically designed for Python. It excels in these areas:

Interactive Coding: Jupyter Notebooks allow you to write, execute, and visualize code in a single document. This makes it ideal for prototyping, experimentation, and exploring AI concepts.

Readability: Code is interspersed with text explanations, equations, and visualizations, enhancing readability and understanding of your AI projects.

Sharing and Collaboration: Jupyter Notebooks are easily shared and collaborative. You can share your notebooks with colleagues for review or use them for educational purposes.

Here's how to get started with Jupyter Notebook:

* Install Jupyter Notebook using `pip install jupyter`.

* Open a terminal and run `jupyter notebook` to launch the web interface.
* You can then create new notebooks and start coding!

2. Exploring Other Development Environments:

While Jupyter Notebook is a popular choice, other development environments cater to different preferences:

PyCharm: A powerful IDE specifically designed for Python development. It offers features like code completion, debugging tools, and integration with version control systems. This is ideal for larger-scale AI projects with complex codebases.

Visual Studio Code: A versatile code editor with various extensions to support Python development effectively. It's lightweight and offers a customizable coding experience. This is a good option for developers familiar with other code editors.

Choosing the Right Environment:

The best development environment depends on your project requirements and preferences. Here's a quick guide:

For beginners or quick experimentation: Jupyter Notebook
For larger-scale projects and complex code: PyCharm

For a customizable and lightweight experience: Visual Studio Code
Ultimately, there's no single "correct" choice. Experiment with different options and see what suits your workflow best!

Part 2: Python Programming Basics

Chapter 4

Variables, Data Types, and Operators

Before venturing into the world of artificial intelligence (AI) with Python, it's crucial to establish a strong foundation in the fundamentals of the language. Here, we'll delve into variables, data types, and operators, the building blocks of any Python program:

1. Variables: Storing Your Data

Variables act as named containers that store data in your Python programs. You can think of them as labeled boxes where you can keep information you want to use later. Here's how to create and use variables:

Assigning a Value: Use the assignment operator (=) to assign a value to a variable. For example:

```Python
name = "Alice"
age = 30
pi = 3.14159
Use code with caution.
content_copy
```

Choosing Variable Names: Variable names should be descriptive and follow Python's naming conventions. They can consist of letters, numbers, and underscores, but cannot start with a number.

2. Data Types: Specifying the Content

Data types define the kind of information a variable can hold. Here are some common data types in Python:

Integers (int): Whole numbers (positive, negative, or zero). Example: age = 30

Floats (float): Numbers with decimal points. Example: pi = 3.14159

Strings (str): Text enclosed in single or double quotes. Example: name = "Alice"

Booleans (bool): Represent logical values: True or False. Example: is_running = True

3. Operators: Performing Calculations and Comparisons

Operators are symbols used to perform operations on variables and values. Here are some essential operators:

*Arithmetic Operators (+, -, , /, //, %): Perform basic mathematical calculations like addition, subtraction, multiplication, division, integer division (gives quotient without remainder), and modulo (remainder after division).

Comparison Operators (==, !=, <, >, <=, >=): Compare values and return True or False based on the condition.

Logical Operators (and, or, not): Combine conditional statements using AND, OR, and NOT operators.

Example:

Python
age = 25
is_adult = age >= 18 # Checks if age is greater than or equal to 18 (True)
Use code with caution.
content_copy

By mastering these core concepts, you'll lay a solid foundation for building more complex Python programs, paving the way for your exploration of

AI. Remember, practice is key! Experiment with different variables, data types, and operators to solidify your understanding.

4.1. Working with numbers, strings, and other data types

Numbers:

Integers (int): Represent whole numbers, positive, negative, or zero. You can perform basic arithmetic operations like addition, subtraction, multiplication, and integer division.

Floats (float): Represent numbers with decimal points. They are used for more precise calculations compared to integers.

Python

```python
# Example: Working with numbers
age = 30  # Integer
pi = 3.14159  # Float

# Arithmetic operations
area_of_circle = pi * (5 ** 2)  # Using multiplication
and exponent
```
Use code with caution.

content_copy

Strings:

Strings (str): Represent sequences of text characters. You can enclose them in single quotes ('), double quotes ("") or triple quotes (''' or """) for multi-line strings. Strings are used for storing and manipulating text data.

Python

```python
# Example: Working with strings
name = "Alice"
greeting = "Hello, " + name  # String concatenation
```

```python
# Accessing characters:
first_letter = name[0]    # Accessing the first
character (A)
```
Use code with caution.

content_copy

Other Data Types:

Booleans (bool): Represent logical values, True or False. They are often used in conditional statements to control program flow.

```python
Python
# Example: Working with booleans
is_running = True
is_adult = age >= 18  # Checking a condition (True if age is 18 or older)
```
Use code with caution.

content_copy

Lists (list): Represent ordered collections of items. These items can be of different data types (numbers, strings, even other lists). Lists are enclosed in square brackets [].

Python
# Example: Working with lists
fruits = ["apple", "banana", "orange"]
first_fruit = fruits[0] # Accessing the first element (apple)
Use code with caution.
content_copy

Tuples (tuple): Similar to lists, but they are immutable, meaning their elements cannot be changed after creation. Tuples are enclosed in parentheses ().

Python
Example: Working with tuples

```python
coordinates = (10, 20)     # Cannot modify
coordinates[0] after creation
```

Use code with caution.

content_copy

Dictionaries (dict): Represent unordered collections of key-value pairs. Keys must be unique and immutable (strings are often used). Values can be of any data type. Dictionaries are enclosed in curly braces {}.

Python
```python
# Example: Working with dictionaries
person = {
    "name": "Bob",
    "age": 42,
    "city": "New York"
}


# Accessing values using keys
```

```
person_name = person["name"]  # Accessing value
for key "name"
```
Use code with caution.

content_copy

By understanding these fundamental data types and how to work with them, you'll be well on your way to writing Python programs that can process and manipulate various kinds of information. Remember to practice using these data types with different operations to solidify your grasp of these core concepts.

4.2. Performing calculations and comparisons

Python empowers you to perform calculations and comparisons on data, essential skills for building intelligent applications, including those in artificial intelligence (AI). Here's a closer look at these functionalities:

1. Calculations: Numerical Gymnastics with Operators

Python provides a rich set of operators to perform various mathematical operations on numbers:

Arithmetic Operators:

+: Addition

-: Subtraction

*: Multiplication

/: Division (results in a float)

//: Integer Division (gives the quotient without remainder)

%: Modulo (remainder after division)

Python

```
# Example: Performing arithmetic operations
price = 10.50
quantity = 2
```

```python
total_cost = price * quantity  # Multiplication (total cost)
discount = 0.1  # Discount rate (float)
discounted_price = price * (1 - discount)  # Combining multiplication and subtraction
```
Use code with caution.

content_copy

Exponential Operator:

**: Exponentiation (a raised to the power of b)

Python

```python
# Example: Calculating area of a square
side_length = 5
area = side_length ** 2  # Square the side length
```
Use code with caution.

content_copy

2. Comparisons: Making Judgments with Relational Operators

Relational operators help you compare values and return Boolean results (True or False):

==: Equal to

!=: Not equal to

<: Less than

>: Greater than

<=: Less than or equal to

>=: Greater than or equal to

Python

```python
# Example: Checking eligibility for a reward
program
age = 22
minimum_age = 18
is_eligible = age >= minimum_age  # True if age is
18 or older
```

Use code with caution.

content_copy

3. Combining Calculations and Comparisons: Building Complex Expressions

You can combine operators to create more complex expressions:

Python
```
# Example: Calculating shipping cost based on
weight
weight = 1.5  # Weight in kilograms
base_cost = 5
cost_per_kg = 2
if weight > 1:
    # Apply additional cost for exceeding base weight
        shipping_cost = base_cost + (weight - 1) *
cost_per_kg
else:
    shipping_cost = base_cost

print(f"Shipping cost: ${shipping_cost}")
```
Use code with caution.

content_copy

Tips for Effective Calculations and Comparisons:

Use parentheses () to control the order of operations (PEMDAS applies).

Consider data types when performing calculations (mixing integers and floats can lead to unexpected results).

Choose meaningful variable names to enhance code readability.

By mastering these calculation and comparison techniques, you'll be equipped to handle various data manipulations in your Python programs, forming a strong foundation for your AI endeavors. Remember, practice is key! Experiment with different operators and expressions to solidify your understanding.

Chapter 5

Control Flow Statements

In any programming language, controlling the flow of execution is essential. Python offers a robust set of control flow statements that dictate how your program progresses. Here's a breakdown of some key statements:

1. Conditional Statements: Making Decisions

if statement: Executes a block of code if a specified condition is True.
Python

```
age = 15
if age >= 18:
    print("You are eligible to vote.")
else:
    print("You are not eligible to vote yet.")
```

Use code with caution.

content_copy

elif statement: Provides additional conditions to check after an initial if statement.

Python

```python
grade = 85
if grade >= 90:
    print("Excellent!")
elif grade >= 80:
    print("Very good!")
else:
    print("Keep practicing!")
```

Use code with caution.

content_copy

else statement: Executes code if none of the preceding conditions in an if or elif statement are True.

2. Looping Statements: Repetitive Tasks Made Easy

for loop: Iterates over a sequence of items (like a list or string).

Python

```
fruits = ["apple", "banana", "cherry"]
for fruit in fruits:
    print(f"I like {fruit}.")
```

Use code with caution.

content_copy

while loop: Executes a block of code as long as a specified condition is True.

Python

```
count = 0
while count < 5:
    print(count)
    count += 1  # Incrementing the counter
```

Use code with caution.

content_copy

3. Break and Continue Statements: Controlling Loop Flow

break statement: Exits a loop prematurely when encountered.

Python

```python
for number in range(1, 11):
    if number == 5:
        break  # Exit the loop when number reaches 5
    print(number)
```

Use code with caution.

content_copy

continue statement: Skips the current iteration of the loop and proceeds to the next.

Python

```python
for letter in "hello":
    if letter == "l":
        continue  # Skip printing the letter "l"
    print(letter)
```

Use code with caution.

content_copy

4. Pass Statement: A Placeholder

pass statement: Does nothing but acts as a placeholder, typically used to maintain the structure of your code when a statement is syntactically required but no action needs to be taken at that point.

Python

```
# Example: An if statement without an actual block of code
if age < 18:
    pass  # Placeholder for future implementation
```

Use code with caution.

content_copy

By understanding and effectively using these control flow statements, you can guide your Python programs to make decisions, repeat tasks, and handle specific conditions, making your code more dynamic and adaptable. As you delve into AI, these statements will be instrumental in building intelligent algorithms that can react to different scenarios and data.

5.1. Using conditional statements (if/else)

Conditional statements, specifically if and else, are the cornerstones of decision-making in Python. They allow your program to execute different blocks of code based on whether a certain condition is True or False. Here's a breakdown of how to use them effectively:

1. The if Statement: Executing Code Based on a Condition

The if statement checks a condition. If the condition evaluates to True, the indented block of code following the if statement is executed.

Python

```python
age = 25
if age >= 18:
    print("You are eligible to vote.")
```

Use code with caution.

content_copy

2. The else Statement: Executing Alternative Code

The else statement provides an alternative block of code to execute if the condition in the if statement is False.

Python

```python
age = 15
if age >= 18:
    print("You are eligible to vote.")
else:
    print("You are not eligible to vote yet.")
```

Use code with caution.

content_copy

3. Chaining if and else Statements (elif):

You can chain multiple conditions using elif (else if) statements. These are checked sequentially after the initial if statement. The first elif condition that evaluates to True will have its corresponding code block executed, and the rest of the elif and else statements are skipped.

```Python
grade = 85
if grade >= 90:
    print("Excellent!")
elif grade >= 80:
    print("Very good!")
else:
    print("Keep practicing!")
```
Use code with caution.
content_copy

4. Nesting if Statements:

You can nest if statements within other if or else blocks to create more complex decision-making logic.

```python
Python
age = 12
is_member = True

if age >= 13:
    if is_member:
        print("You can participate in the advanced competition.")
    else:
        print("You can join the regular competition after becoming a member.")
else:
    print("You can join the junior competition.")
Use code with caution.
content_copy
```

Tips for Effective Conditional Statements:

Use clear and concise variable names to improve code readability.

Indentation is crucial in Python. Make sure your code blocks are properly indented to define their scope.

Break down complex logic into smaller, more manageable if statements for better maintainability.

Consider using comments to explain the purpose of your conditional statements, especially for nested structures.

By mastering conditional statements, you'll equip your Python programs with the ability to make decisions and respond to different conditions. This is essential for building intelligent applications in various domains, including AI.

5.2. Using loops (for/while)

Loops are fundamental building blocks in Python, allowing you to execute a block of code repeatedly until a certain condition is met. Here, we'll explore two prominent loop types: for and while.

1. for loop: Iterating Over Sequences

The for loop is ideal for iterating over a sequence of items, such as a list, string, or tuple. Here's how it works:

```python
Python
fruits = ["apple", "banana", "cherry"]
for fruit in fruits:
    print(f"I like {fruit}.")
Use code with caution.
content_copy
```

In this example:

fruits is the sequence we want to iterate over.

fruit is the loop variable that takes on the value of each item in the sequence during each iteration.

The indented block of code following the for statement is executed for each item in the sequence.

2. while loop: Repeating Until a Condition is Met

The while loop continues executing a block of code as long as a specified condition is True. This allows for more flexible control over the number of iterations.

Python

```python
count = 0
while count < 5:
    print(count)
    count += 1  # Incrementing the counter
```

Use code with caution.

content_copy

Here:

count is a variable that keeps track of the number of iterations.

The condition count < 5 checks if count is less than 5.

The loop keeps executing as long as the condition is True (until count reaches 5).

Inside the loop, count is incremented by 1 to ensure the loop eventually terminates.

3. break and continue Statements: Controlling Loop Flow

break statement: Exits the loop prematurely when encountered.

Python

```python
for number in range(1, 11):
    if number == 5:
        break  # Exit the loop when number reaches 5
    print(number)
```

Use code with caution.

content_copy

continue statement: Skips the current iteration of the loop and proceeds to the next.

Python
```python
for letter in "hello":
    if letter == "l":
        continue  # Skip printing the letter "l"
    print(letter)
```
Use code with caution.

content_copy

Choosing the Right Loop:

Use for loops when you know the exact number of times you want to iterate or when you're working with a sequence of items.

Use while loops when you don't know the exact number of iterations beforehand, and the loop's continuation depends on a condition.

Beyond the Basics:

Loops can be nested to create more complex iteration patterns. Remember to properly indent your code to define the scope of each loop.

By mastering loops, you'll empower your Python programs to automate repetitive tasks, process large datasets efficiently, and build the foundation for iterative algorithms commonly used in AI applications.

5.3. Controlling the flow of your programs

In the realm of programming, controlling the flow of your program's execution is paramount. Python offers a robust set of tools to guide how your code progresses, making it adaptable and responsive.

Here's a roadmap to navigate control flow effectively:

1. Conditional Statements: Making Decisions (if, else, elif)

if statements: The cornerstone of decision-making. They evaluate a condition and execute a block of code if the condition is True.

Python
```
age = 20
if age >= 18:
    print("You are eligible to vote.")
```
Use code with caution.

content_copy

else statements: Provide an alternative path if the if condition is False.

Python
```
is_member = False
if is_member:
```

```
    print("Welcome back, valued member!")
else:
        print("Join our membership for exclusive
benefits.")
```
Use code with caution.

content_copy

elif statements (else if): Allow for chaining multiple conditions after an initial if statement.

Python
```
grade = 87
if grade >= 90:
   print("Excellent work!")
elif grade >= 80:
   print("Very good!")
else:
   print("Keep practicing!")
```
Use code with caution.

content_copy

2. Looping Statements: Automating Repetition (for, while)

for loops: Ideal for iterating over a sequence of items (like a list or string).

Python
```
fruits = ["apple", "banana", "cherry"]
for fruit in fruits:
    print(f"I'm adding {fruit} to the basket.")
```
Use code with caution.

content_copy

while loops: Continue executing a block of code as long as a specified condition is True.

Python
```
count = 1
while count <= 5:
    print(count)
    count += 1  # Incrementing the counter
```

Use code with caution.

content_copy

3. break and continue Statements: Fine-Tuning Loop Flow

break statement: Exits a loop prematurely when encountered.

Python

```
for number in range(1, 11):
    if number == 7:
        break  # Exit the loop when number reaches 7
    print(number)
```

Use code with caution.

content_copy

continue statement: Skips the current iteration of the loop and proceeds to the next.

Python

```
for letter in "hello world":
```

```python
    if letter == " ":
        continue  # Skip printing spaces
    print(letter, end="")  # Printing without a new line
```
Use code with caution.

content_copy

4. Functions: Organizing Code and Promoting Reusability

Functions act as self-contained blocks of code that perform specific tasks. You can define functions and call them from different parts of your program, promoting code organization and reusability.

Python
```python
def greet(name):
    """Prints a greeting message."""
    print(f"Hello, {name}!")


greet("Alice")  # Calling the greet function
```
Use code with caution.

content_copy

5. Error Handling: Anticipating and Gracefully Addressing Issues

try...except block: Allows you to handle potential errors (exceptions) that might occur during program execution.

Python
```
try:
  result = 10 / 0  # This will cause a division by zero
error
except ZeroDivisionError:
  print("Oops! Cannot divide by zero.")
```
Use code with caution.

content_copy

Chapter 6

Functions and Modules

.

In the world of Python programming, functions and modules are essential building blocks that promote code organization, reusability, and efficiency. Here's a breakdown of their roles:

Functions: Encapsulating Reusable Code Blocks

A function is a named block of code that performs a specific task. It promotes code reusability by allowing you to define a task once and call it from different parts of your program or even other Python programs.

Functions can take parameters (inputs) and return values (outputs) to customize their behavior.

Python

```
def greet(name):
```

```
"""Prints a greeting message."""
print(f"Hello, {name}!")


greet("Alice")  # Calling the greet function with an
argument
```
Use code with caution.

content_copy

Benefits of Using Functions:

Improved Code Readability: Functions break down complex programs into smaller, more manageable blocks, making code easier to understand and maintain.

Reduced Redundancy: By defining a task in a function, you can avoid duplicating code for repetitive actions.

Modularity: Functions promote modular programming, where you can organize your code into logical units.

Modules: Grouping Related Functions and Variables

A module is a Python file containing functions, variables, and classes. It allows you to group related functionalities together, promoting organization and reusability across different programs.

You can import modules into your Python programs to access the functions and variables they define.

Python

```python
# In a module named math_utils.py
def add(x, y):
  """Returns the sum of x and y."""
  return x + y


# In your main program
import math_utils

result = math_utils.add(5, 3)
```

```
print(result)  # Output: 8
```
Use code with caution.

content_copy

Using Modules Effectively:

Importing Specific Functions: You can import specific functions from a module using the from ... import syntax.

Python
```
from math_utils import add

result = add(7, 2)
print(result)  # Output: 9
```
Use code with caution.

content_copy

Importing Entire Modules: Use the import statement to import all functions and variables from a module, but be cautious of naming conflicts with built-in functions or variables.

The Standard Library: A Rich Collection of Modules

Python comes with a vast standard library containing modules for various tasks, like file handling, networking, mathematical computations, and more. This saves you time by providing pre-written, well-tested code.

By effectively utilizing functions and modules, you'll structure your Python programs for clarity, maintainability, and reusability – essential qualities for building robust and scalable applications, including those in artificial intelligence (AI).

Remember, as you venture into AI, you'll encounter libraries specifically designed for machine learning and deep learning tasks, leveraging these core concepts to create intelligent systems.

6.1. Defining reusable blocks of code (functions)

In Python, functions are the workhorses that take care of specific tasks within your program. They encapsulate a block of code, allowing you to reuse it throughout your program or even in other Python programs. Here's a breakdown of how to define and use functions effectively:

1. Creating a Function: The def Keyword

You use the def keyword to define a function. Here's the basic structure:

Python

```python
def function_name(parameters):
  """Docstring (optional)"""
  # Function body ( indented block of code)
  return output  # Optional return value
```

Use code with caution.

content_copy

function_name: A unique name that identifies your function. Choose a descriptive name that reflects what the function does.

parameters (optional): A comma-separated list of variables that the function accepts as input. These are used within the function's body to perform its task.

Docstring (optional): A brief explanation of what the function does and how to use it. This improves code readability and maintainability.

Function body: The indented block of code that defines the function's logic and operations.

return (optional): A statement that specifies the value the function returns after its execution. If no return statement is present, the function returns None by default.

2. Calling a Function: Putting It to Work

Once you've defined a function, you can call it from other parts of your program using its name followed by parentheses. You can optionally pass arguments (values) when calling the function, which correspond to the parameters defined in the function's signature.

Python
```
def greet(name):
  """Prints a greeting message."""
  print(f"Hello, {name}!")


greet("Alice")  # Calling the greet function with an argument
```
Use code with caution.
content_copy

3. Benefits of Using Functions:

Reusability: The core benefit of functions is that you can define a task once and use it multiple times throughout your code or even in different programs. This saves time and effort by avoiding code duplication.

Readability: Functions break down complex programs into smaller, more manageable blocks, making code easier to understand and maintain for yourself and others.

Modularity: Functions promote modular programming, where you can organize your code into logical units based on functionality. This improves code organization and maintainability.

4. Example: Using a Function with Calculations

Python
```python
def calculate_area(length, width):
  """Calculates the area of a rectangle."""
  area = length * width
  return area
```

```
rectangle_area = calculate_area(5, 3)  # Calling the
function with arguments
print(f"The     area     of     the     rectangle     is
{rectangle_area}.")
```
Use code with caution.

content_copy

6.2. Importing and using code from external modules

The Python world extends beyond your individual programs. Modules, also called libraries or packages, store reusable code written by others. This allows you to import functionalities you need without reinventing the wheel. Here's how to harness the power of external modules:

1. Installation: Bringing Modules into Your Environment

Most useful modules aren't part of the Python standard library by default. You'll typically install them using a package manager like pip:

Bash
pip install module_name
Use code with caution.
content_copy
This downloads and installs the module and its dependencies into your Python environment.

2. Importing Modules: Making External Code Accessible

Once a module is installed, you can import it into your program using the import statement:

Python

```
import module_name
```
Use code with caution.

content_copy

This makes the module's functions, variables, and classes available for use in your program.

3. Using Functions from Modules:

Once you've imported a module, you can access its functions using dot notation:

Python
```
import math

# Calling a function from the math module
result = math.sqrt(16)   # Using the square root function
print(result) # Output: 4.0
```
Use code with caution.

content_copy

4. Importing Specific Functions:

If you only need a few functions from a module, you can import them directly:

Python
```
from math import sqrt, pi

# Using the imported functions
area_of_circle = pi * (radius**2)   # Using pi and assuming radius is defined
```
Use code with caution.
content_copy

5. Standard Library vs. Third-Party Modules:

Standard Library: Python comes with a rich collection of built-in modules for various tasks like file handling, networking, and data structures. These are readily available without installation (e.g., math, os, random).

Third-Party Modules: The Python Package Index (PyPI) offers a vast repository of third-party modules for specialized functionalities like machine learning, web scraping, data analysis, and more. You'll need to install these using pip.

6. Tips for Effective Module Usage:

Choose Clear and Descriptive Names: When importing functions directly, avoid using overly generic names that might conflict with built-in functions.

Document Your Code: Clearly state which modules you're using and why. This improves code readability and maintainability.
Stay Updated: Third-party modules are frequently updated, so consider using tools like pip freeze to check for and manage updates.

By effectively importing and using modules, you'll gain access to a vast ecosystem of pre-written, well-tested code, saving you time and effort. This is especially crucial in AI, where numerous libraries are specifically designed for machine learning and deep learning tasks. Remember, as you explore AI, effectively leveraging modules will be instrumental in building intelligent and efficient systems.

Part 3: Machine Learning Fundamentals

Chapter 7

Introduction to Machine Learning

Machine learning (ML) is a fascinating subfield of artificial intelligence (AI) that empowers computers to learn without being explicitly programmed. Imagine a program that can improve its performance on a task through experience, just like humans do! That's the core idea behind machine learning. Here's a glimpse into this captivating domain:

1. The Core Concept: Learning from Data

Unlike traditional programming, where you provide step-by-step instructions, machine learning algorithms learn from data. This data can be anything from numbers and text to images and videos. By analyzing patterns and relationships within the data, the algorithm improves its ability to perform a specific task.

2. Types of Machine Learning:

Supervised Learning: The algorithm is trained on labeled data, where each data point has a corresponding label (correct answer). The goal is to learn from these labeled examples and make accurate predictions for new, unseen data.

Example: An email spam filter is trained on labeled emails (spam and not spam) to identify future spam emails.

Unsupervised Learning: The algorithm discovers hidden patterns in unlabeled data, where data points lack predefined labels. It aims to group similar data points together or find underlying structures within the data.

Example: Recommender systems analyze your past purchases or browsing history to suggest products you might be interested in.

Reinforcement Learning: The algorithm learns through trial and error in an interactive environment. It receives rewards for desired actions and penalties for undesired ones, constantly refining its behavior to maximize rewards.

Example: An AI agent playing a game learns through trial and error, experimenting with different strategies to achieve the goal of winning the game.

3. Common Machine Learning Applications:

Machine learning has revolutionized various fields:

Image Recognition: Facial recognition in photos, self-driving cars identifying objects on the road.

Natural Language Processing (NLP): Machine translation, chatbots understanding and responding to human language.

Recommendation Systems: Suggesting products, movies, or music based on your preferences.

Fraud Detection: Identifying suspicious financial transactions that might be fraudulent.

Scientific Discovery: Analyzing large datasets to uncover hidden patterns and accelerate research.

4. Getting Started with Machine Learning:

Python: The most popular language for machine learning due to its extensive libraries like scikit-learn, TensorFlow, and PyTorch.

Learn the Basics: Grasp fundamental programming concepts like variables, data types, and control flow before diving into machine learning algorithms.

Online Resources: Numerous online courses, tutorials, and communities can guide your learning journey.

Machine learning opens a world of possibilities for building intelligent systems that can learn and adapt. As you delve deeper, you'll explore various algorithms, techniques, and tools to create your own intelligent applications.

7.1. Understanding the core concepts of machine learning

, here's a breakdown of the core concepts in machine learning:

1. The Learning Paradigm: Shifting from Explicit Programming

Traditionally, programmers write detailed instructions for computers to follow. Machine learning flips this paradigm. Here, algorithms learn from data, enabling them to improve performance on a specific task without explicit programming for every situation.

2. Data: The Fuel for Learning

Data is the lifeblood of machine learning. It can be structured (numbers in tables) or unstructured (text, images, videos). The quality and quantity of data significantly impact the effectiveness of machine learning models.

3. Algorithms: The Learning Engines

Machine learning algorithms are mathematical models that analyze data and identify patterns. These patterns are then used to make predictions or decisions on new, unseen data. Here are some common algorithm categories:

Supervised Learning: The algorithm is trained on labeled data, where each data point has a corresponding label (correct answer). For example, a spam filter is trained on labeled emails (spam and not spam) to identify future spam.

Unsupervised Learning: The algorithm discovers patterns in unlabeled data, where data points lack predefined labels. It aims to group similar data points together or find underlying structures within the data. For instance, recommender systems analyze your past purchases to suggest products you might be interested in.

Reinforcement Learning: The algorithm learns through trial and error in an interactive environment. It receives rewards for desired actions and penalties for undesired ones, constantly refining its behavior to maximize rewards. Imagine an AI agent playing a game; it learns by experimenting with different strategies to win.

4. The Training Process: Feeding Data to the Algorithm

The training process involves feeding the machine learning algorithm a representative dataset. The algorithm analyzes the data, learns from the patterns, and builds a model. This model can then be used to make predictions or decisions on new data.

5. Evaluation: Measuring Performance

Once trained, a machine learning model needs to be evaluated to assess its effectiveness. This involves testing the model on unseen data and measuring how well it performs on the task it's designed for. Common metrics include accuracy, precision, recall, and F1-score.

6. Prediction and Decision Making:

The ultimate goal of machine learning is to make predictions or decisions based on the learned patterns from data. For instance, a spam filter predicts whether an email is spam, or a recommendation system recommends products you might like.

7. Model Optimization: Refining the Learner

Machine learning models are rarely perfect. Techniques like hyperparameter tuning and regularization can be used to improve the model's performance by adjusting its internal parameters or reducing overfitting (memorizing the training data too closely).

By understanding these core concepts, you'll be well on your way to grasping the essence of machine learning and its potential to revolutionize various fields. As you progress, you'll explore specific algorithms, delve deeper into different data types, and discover the exciting world of building intelligent applications that can learn and adapt over time.

7.2. Supervised vs. Unsupervised learning

In the realm of machine learning, choosing the right learning approach is crucial. Two fundamental categories dominate the landscape: supervised and unsupervised learning. Here's a breakdown to help you understand their distinctions:

Supervised Learning: Learning with a Teacher (Labeled Data)

Imagine a student learning with a teacher's guidance. In supervised learning, the algorithm acts like the student, and the data acts as the teacher.

Labeled Data: The core principle of supervised learning is labeled data. Each data point has a corresponding label or correct answer. This labeled data serves as the guide for the algorithm to learn from.

Training Process: The labeled data is used to train the algorithm. The algorithm analyzes the data, including the features (input variables) and the target variables (labels), and builds a model that maps the features to the target variables.

Common Tasks: Prediction, classification, regression.

Examples:

Spam filter: Trained on labeled emails (spam and not spam) to categorize new emails.

Image recognition: Trained on labeled images (cat, dog, etc.) to identify objects in new images.

Weather prediction: Trained on historical weather data with labels (sunny, rainy, etc.) to predict future weather patterns.

Unsupervised Learning: Finding Hidden Patterns on Your Own (Unlabeled Data)

Unlike supervised learning, unsupervised learning doesn't have a teacher or labeled data. It's like exploring a new environment and discovering patterns on your own.

Unlabeled Data: The algorithm is presented with unlabeled data, where data points lack predefined labels. The goal is to uncover hidden patterns or structures within this data.

Common Tasks: Clustering, dimensionality reduction, anomaly detection.

Examples:

Recommender systems: Analyze your purchase history to recommend products you might be interested in (no labels indicating what you'll buy).

Market segmentation: Group customers with similar characteristics based on their purchase behavior (no labels for customer segments).

Anomaly detection: Identify unusual patterns in sensor data that might indicate potential equipment failure (no labels for "normal" vs. "anomalous" data).

Choosing the Right Approach:

If you have labeled data and a well-defined prediction task (e.g., classifying emails as spam or not spam), supervised learning is a good choice.

If you have unlabeled data and want to explore patterns or group similar data points, unsupervised learning is the way to go.

In essence, supervised learning excels at structured tasks with labeled data, while unsupervised learning shines in uncovering hidden structures and patterns from unlabeled data. As you venture into machine learning, understanding these core concepts will empower you to select the most suitable approach for your specific problem and data.

Chapter 8

Data Preparation and Exploration

In the world of machine learning, data is king. But raw data isn't enough. Before you unleash the power of machine learning algorithms, data preparation and exploration are essential steps to lay a solid foundation for your project. Here's why they matter:

1. Data Preparation: Cleaning and Shaping Your Raw Material

Imagine building a house on a shaky foundation. Data preparation is akin to preparing the ground for your machine learning model. It involves cleaning, transforming, and manipulating your raw data to ensure it's suitable for analysis and modeling. Here are some key aspects:

Handling Missing Values: Missing data points are a common occurrence. You might need to decide to impute them with estimates, remove rows/columns with excessive missingness, or adopt other strategies.

Dealing with Outliers: Extreme values (outliers) can skew your results. You might need to identify and handle them appropriately, such as winsorizing (capping outliers to a certain threshold).

Encoding Categorical Data: Machine learning algorithms typically work with numerical data. You might need to encode categorical variables (like text labels) into numerical representations.
Feature Scaling: Features (input variables) can have different scales. Scaling them to a common range can improve the performance of some machine learning algorithms.

2. Data Exploration: Understanding What Your Data Tells You

Data exploration is like examining a map before embarking on a journey. It helps you understand the characteristics of your data, identify potential issues, and gain insights that can guide your modeling decisions. Here's what you might explore:

Central Tendency: Measures like mean, median, and mode summarize the "center" of your data distribution.

Distribution of Features: Visualizations like histograms and boxplots reveal how your data is spread out for each feature.

Relationships Between Features: Techniques like correlation analysis can help uncover relationships between different features in your data.

3. Tools for Data Preparation and Exploration

Python libraries like Pandas, NumPy, and scikit-learn offer a rich set of tools for data manipulation, cleaning, and exploration. Visualization libraries like Matplotlib and Seaborn help you create informative plots and charts to understand your data visually.

4. Benefits of Data Preparation and Exploration:

Improved Model Performance: Clean and well-prepared data leads to more accurate and robust machine learning models.
Reduced Training Time: Proper data preparation can streamline the training process for your algorithms.

Feature Engineering Opportunities: Exploration can reveal potential for creating new features from existing data, potentially improving model performance.

Early Detection of Issues: Data exploration can help you identify problems like biases or inconsistencies in your data before they impact your models.

By investing time in data preparation and exploration, you'll equip your machine learning projects with a solid foundation for success. Remember, "garbage in, garbage out" applies to machine learning as well. Clean, well-understood data is the fuel that powers effective models.

8.1. Loading and cleaning data for machine learning tasks

In the realm of machine learning, data is the lifeblood. But before you unleash its potential, wrangling raw data into a usable format is crucial.

Loading and cleaning data are the initial steps that prepare your data for building robust machine learning models. Here's a roadmap to navigate this essential process:

1. Loading Your Data: Importing from Various Sources

The Gateway: The first step is to load your data into your machine learning environment. This involves using libraries like Pandas in Python to import data from various sources:

CSV Files: The most common format for structured data, loaded using pandas.read_csv().
JSON Files: Another popular format for semi-structured data, loaded using pandas.read_json().

Databases: You can connect to databases using libraries like SQLAlchemy to retrieve data for your models.

2. Exploring Your Data: Getting to Know What You Have

A Sneak Peek: Once loaded, take some time to explore your data. This helps identify potential issues and understand its characteristics:

Data Types: Examine the data types of each feature (column) to ensure they align with what your machine learning model expects (e.g., numerical features for mathematical operations).

Missing Values: Check for missing data points and decide on a strategy to handle them (removal, imputation with estimates, etc.).

Descriptive Statistics: Calculate summary statistics like mean, median, and standard deviation to understand the central tendency and spread of your data.

3. Data Cleaning: Addressing Imperfections

The Refinement Process: Raw data often contains inconsistencies, errors, and missing values that can hinder your machine learning model's performance.

Data cleaning tackles these issues:
Handling Missing Values: Decide on an appropriate strategy based on the extent and distribution of missingness. You can remove rows with excessive missing values, impute missing values with estimates (mean, median), or use more sophisticated techniques.

Dealing with Outliers: Extreme values (outliers) can skew your results. You might need to identify and handle them appropriately, such as winsorizing (capping outliers to a certain threshold) or removing them if they are truly erroneous.

Encoding Categorical Data: Machine learning algorithms typically work with numerical data. You'll need to encode categorical variables (like text labels) into numerical representations using techniques like one-hot encoding or label encoding. Formatting and Standardization: Ensure consistent formatting across your data (e.g., date format, capitalization). Consider feature scaling if features have different ranges to improve the performance of some machine learning algorithms.

4. Tools for Loading and Cleaning Data

Your Allies in the Wrangling Process: Python libraries like Pandas and scikit-learn provide a powerful toolkit for data manipulation and cleaning:

Pandas: Offers functions for data loading (e.g., read_csv()), exploration (e.g., describe()), cleaning

(e.g., fillna(), dropna()), and transformation (e.g., get_dummies() for one-hot encoding).
Scikit-learn: Provides tools for data preprocessing tasks like scaling features (e.g., StandardScaler()) and handling missing values (e.g., SimpleImputer()).

5. Benefits of Clean Data:

Improved Model Performance: Clean and well-prepared data leads to more accurate and robust machine learning models.
Reduced Training Time: Proper data cleaning can streamline the training process for your algorithms.
Feature Engineering Opportunities: Cleaning may reveal potential for creating new features from existing data, potentially improving model performance.

Early Detection of Issues: Data exploration during cleaning can help you identify problems like biases or inconsistencies in your data before they impact your models.

Remember, data loading and cleaning are the foundation for successful machine learning projects. By investing time in these steps, you'll ensure your models are built on a solid and reliable base, ultimately leading to better results.

8.2. Visualizing and analyzing data

In the realm of machine learning, data is king, but raw data can be like a treasure chest locked tight. Data visualization and analysis are the keys that unlock its secrets, enabling you to extract valuable insights and make informed decisions for your machine learning models.

1. Data Visualization: Shedding Light on Patterns

The human brain excels at processing visual information. Data visualization translates complex data into graphical representations, revealing patterns, trends, and relationships that might be difficult to discern from raw numbers. Here are some common data visualization techniques for machine learning:

Histograms: Illustrate the distribution of data for a single numerical feature.

Scatter Plots: Reveal relationships between two numerical features.

Box Plots: Depict the distribution of data for a numerical feature, highlighting the median, quartiles, and outliers.
Heatmaps: Visualize the strength of correlations between multiple features.

2. Data Analysis: Delving Deeper with Statistical Methods

Data visualization provides a high-level view, but data analysis techniques offer a more rigorous approach to understanding your data. Here are some core concepts:

Central Tendency: Measures like mean, median, and mode summarize the "center" of your data distribution.

Variability: Measures like standard deviation and interquartile range (IQR) quantify how spread out your data is.

Correlation Analysis: Calculates the correlation coefficient to assess the strength and direction of the linear relationship between two features.

3. Tools for Data Visualization and Analysis

Python libraries like Pandas, Matplotlib, Seaborn, and scikit-learn provide a comprehensive set of tools for data exploration and analysis:

Pandas: Offers functionalities for data exploration (e.g., describe()) and data cleaning (e.g., corr() for correlation analysis).

Matplotlib and Seaborn: Provide extensive functionalities for creating various plots and charts like histograms, scatter plots, and heatmaps.

Scikit-learn: Offers statistical functions for calculating measures of central tendency (e.g., mean()) and variability (e.g., StandardScaler() for standardization).

4. Benefits of Data Visualization and Analysis:

Improved Feature Engineering: Visualization and analysis can help identify redundant features or suggest the creation of new features from existing ones to improve model performance.

Early Detection of Biases: Data exploration can reveal potential biases in your data that might impact your machine learning models.

Model Selection and Evaluation: Understanding your data's characteristics helps you choose appropriate machine learning algorithms and evaluate their performance effectively.

5. Visualization and Analysis in Action:

Identifying outliers: Box plots can help identify outliers that might skew your machine learning model's results.

Visualizing feature relationships: Scatter plots can reveal linear relationships between features, which might be beneficial for algorithms like linear regression.

Understanding feature distributions: Histograms can expose skewed data distributions, which might require specific preprocessing techniques before feeding the data to your model.

In conclusion, data visualization and analysis are powerful tools for any machine learning project. By effectively using these techniques, you'll unlock the hidden potential within your data, enabling you to build more accurate and robust machine learning models.

Chapter 9

Machine Learning Algorithms

In the captivating world of machine learning, algorithms are the workhorses that unveil patterns and insights from data. These algorithms are mathematical models that can learn from data, allowing them to make predictions or decisions on new, unseen data. Here's a glimpse into some of the most common machine learning algorithms:

1. Classification: Sorting Things Into Categories

Classification algorithms are like intelligent sorting machines. They learn to categorize data points into predefined classes. Here are some popular examples:

Logistic Regression: A fundamental algorithm for binary classification (two classes), predicting the probability of an instance belonging to a specific class. For instance, it can be used to classify emails as spam or not spam.

K-Nearest Neighbors (KNN): Classifies a data point based on the majority vote of its k nearest neighbors in the training data. Imagine classifying an image of an animal based on the most similar animals (neighbors) it has in the training data (e.g., cats, dogs).

Support Vector Machines (SVM): Aims to create a clear separation hyperplane between different classes in the data. It's particularly useful for high-dimensional data and when dealing with clear class boundaries.

2. Regression: Unveiling Relationships and Making Predictions

Regression algorithms delve into the world of continuous values. They learn the relationship between input features and a continuous output variable, enabling them to make predictions for new data points. Here are some common types:

Linear Regression: Discovers the linear relationship between features and a continuous target variable. Imagine predicting house prices based on size, location, and other numerical features.

Decision Trees: These tree-like models use a series of branching questions based on features to predict a continuous output value. They are interpretable, making it easier to understand the decision-making process.

Random Forest: Combines the power of multiple decision trees, reducing the variance and improving prediction accuracy. Think of it as a forest (ensemble) of decision trees voting together for a more robust prediction.

3. Clustering: Grouping Similar Data Points

Clustering algorithms are like automatic organizers, grouping similar data points together without predefined categories. Here's a common approach:

K-Means Clustering: Identifies a predefined number (k) of clusters in the data by strategically placing centroids (cluster centers) and assigning data points to the closest centroid. Imagine grouping customers with similar purchase history into different segments.

4. Choosing the Right Algorithm: A Match for Every Task

The selection of a machine learning algorithm depends on the nature of your problem and data:

Classification vs. Regression: For tasks with predefined categories, choose classification algorithms. For predicting continuous values, choose regression algorithms.

Supervised vs. Unsupervised Learning: If you have labeled data, supervised learning algorithms are a good choice. If your data is unlabeled, explore unsupervised learning options.

Data Characteristics: Consider factors like data dimensionality (number of features) and linearity of relationships between features when selecting algorithms.

5. Beyond the Basics: A Universe of Algorithms

The world of machine learning algorithms extends far beyond these core examples. Deep learning algorithms, inspired by the structure and function of the brain, are revolutionizing fields like computer vision and natural language processing. As you venture further into machine learning, you'll explore a diverse landscape of algorithms, each with its strengths and applications.

By understanding these fundamental algorithms and their purposes, you'll be well-equipped to tackle various machine learning challenges.

Remember, the key is to identify the problem you're trying to solve and select the algorithm that best suits your data and task.

9.1. Introduction to common algorithms (linear regression, decision trees)

In the realm of machine learning, algorithms are the intelligent engines that unlock the secrets hidden within data. Two of the most fundamental and versatile algorithms you'll encounter are linear regression and decision trees. Let's delve into their capabilities:

1. Linear Regression: Predicting Continuous Values with a Straight Line

Imagine you want to predict house prices based on factors like size and location. Linear regression comes in handy for this task. It's a supervised learning algorithm that learns the linear relationship between one or more independent variables (features, like house size) and a dependent variable (continuous output, like house price).

Core Idea: Linear regression finds a straight line (or hyperplane in higher dimensions) that best fits the data points. The equation of this line allows you to predict the output value for new unseen data points.

Applications: Beyond house prices, linear regression is used in various domains like stock price prediction, sales forecasting, and understanding relationships between economic indicators.

2. Decision Trees: Making Predictions Through a Series of Questions

Think of a decision tree like a flowchart you use to make decisions. In machine learning, decision tree algorithms use a tree-like structure to classify data or predict a continuous value.

Working Principle: The algorithm starts at the root node and asks a series of questions based on the features of the data. Depending on the answer (Yes/No or specific value range), it traverses the tree, reaching a leaf node that holds the final prediction (class label or continuous value).

Advantages: Decision trees are interpretable. You can easily understand the decision-making process by following the branches of the tree. They are also versatile, handling both classification and regression problems.

Applications: Decision trees are used in fraud detection (classifying transactions as fraudulent or legitimate), medical diagnosis (predicting patient outcomes), and loan approval decisions (classifying applicants as high-risk or low-risk).

3. Linear Regression vs. Decision Trees: Choosing the Right Tool

Data Type: Linear regression works best for continuous output variables. Decision trees can handle both classification (categorical output) and regression tasks.

Data Complexity: Linear regression assumes a linear relationship between features and the target variable. Decision trees can capture more complex, non-linear relationships.

Interpretability: Both algorithms offer interpretability, but decision trees are generally considered easier to understand due to their tree-like structure.

4. Conclusion: A Solid Foundation for Machine Learning

Linear regression and decision trees are foundational algorithms in machine learning. By mastering these concepts, you'll gain a strong understanding of how algorithms can learn from data and make predictions. As you progress, you'll explore more advanced algorithms and delve deeper into the fascinating world of machine learning.

9.2. Training and evaluating models

In machine learning, models are like students – they need proper training to excel. This section will unveil the processes of training and evaluating machine learning models, equipping you to create robust and effective models.

1. Training: Feeding Data to the Algorithm

Imagine showing a student a set of practice problems to prepare for an exam. Training a machine learning model follows a similar principle. You provide the algorithm with a training dataset, which represents a subset of your entire data. This dataset includes both input features (independent variables) and the desired output (dependent variable or target variable).

The Learning Process: The algorithm analyzes the training data, identifying patterns and relationships between features and the target variable. Based on this analysis, it builds an internal mathematical model that can map input features to the desired output.

Training Algorithms: Different algorithms have different training procedures. For instance, linear regression uses optimization techniques to find the best-fit line, while decision trees learn by recursively splitting the data based on features.

2. Evaluation: Assessing the Model's Performance

Just as you wouldn't send a student to an exam without testing their knowledge, evaluating a machine learning model is crucial. Here's how we assess a model's effectiveness:

Hold-out Set: A common approach is to split your data into two sets: training and testing. The model is trained on the training set, and its performance is evaluated on the unseen testing set. This helps prevent overfitting, where the model simply memorizes the training data and performs poorly on new data.

Evaluation Metrics: Different metrics are used depending on the task. For classification problems, accuracy, precision, recall, and F1-score are common choices. For regression problems, metrics like mean squared error (MSE) or R-squared are used.

3. The Importance of Evaluation:

Identifying Model Strengths and Weaknesses: Evaluation helps you understand how well your model performs on unseen data, revealing its strengths and weaknesses.

Fine-tuning the Model: Based on the evaluation results, you can fine-tune the model by adjusting hyperparameters (internal settings of the algorithm) or trying different algorithms altogether.

Real-World Applicability: Ultimately, evaluation ensures your model generalizes well to real-world scenarios, making accurate predictions on data it hasn't seen before.

4. Common Challenges in Training and Evaluation

Overfitting: When a model memorizes the training data too closely and performs poorly on unseen data. Techniques like using a hold-out set and regularization can help mitigate this.

Underfitting: When a model fails to capture the underlying patterns in the data, resulting in poor performance on both training and testing data.

Choosing a more complex model or gathering more data can address this.

Data Bias: If your training data is biased, your model will inherit that bias and produce biased predictions. It's crucial to be aware of potential biases in your data and try to mitigate them.

5. Tools for Training and Evaluation

Popular Python libraries like scikit-learn provide functionalities for training and evaluating machine learning models:

scikit-learn: Offers various algorithms with built-in training and evaluation methods. It also provides tools for splitting data into training and testing sets (e.g., train_test_split()) and performance metrics (e.g., accuracy_score() for classification).

By effectively training and evaluating your machine learning models, you'll ensure they are well-equipped to handle real-world challenges and deliver reliable results. As you venture further, you'll explore more sophisticated training techniques and delve deeper into the art of crafting high-performing machine learning models.

Part 4: Building Basic AI Applications with Python

Chapter 10

Building a Simple Recommender System

Recommender systems are a cornerstone of many online experiences, suggesting products, movies, music, or even friends you might like. In essence, they predict what users will be interested in based on their past behavior or preferences. Here's a roadmap to build a simple recommender system:

1. Data Collection: The Foundation of Recommendations

User Data: This is the gold mine for your recommender system. You'll need data on user interactions, such as purchases, ratings, or browsing history.

Item Data: Information about the items you're recommending is essential. This could include product descriptions, genres for movies/music, or features of different items.

2. Collaborative Filtering: Learning from Like-Minded Users

This approach is based on the idea that users with similar tastes tend to like similar items. Here's the workflow:

* **User-Item Matrix:** Create a matrix where rows represent users and columns represent items. Each cell contains a value indicating the user's interaction (e.g., rating or purchase) with an item. Often, this matrix is sparse, with many empty cells.
* **Similarity Measures:** Calculate the similarity between users based on their interaction patterns. Common metrics include cosine similarity or Pearson correlation coefficient.

* **Recommendations:** For a target user, identify similar users based on the similarity measures. Recommend items that these similar users have interacted with but the target user hasn't (assuming they'll be of interest).

3. Content-Based Filtering: Recommending Similar Items

This approach focuses on the item itself, recommending items with similar features to those a user has interacted with in the past. Here's the process:

* **Item Features:** Identify relevant features for your items. For instance, movie features could include genre, director, or actors.
* **Item Similarity:** Calculate the similarity between items based on their features. You can use techniques like Jaccard similarity or cosine similarity.

* **Recommendations:** For a target user, recommend items that are similar to items they have interacted with in the past.

4. Hybrid Approaches: The Best of Both Worlds

Combining collaborative filtering and content-based filtering can often outperform either approach alone. This leverages the strengths of both methods:

* **Collaborative filtering captures user preferences beyond item features.**
* **Content-based filtering addresses cold start problems (when new items lack user interaction data) by recommending similar items based on features.**

5. Simple Recommendation System in Python

Here's a glimpse of how you might implement a simple recommender system using Python libraries like Pandas and NumPy:

Python

```python
# Sample user-item matrix (replace with your data)
user_item_matrix = ...

# Calculate user similarities (cosine similarity)
from sklearn.metrics.pairwise import cosine_similarity
user_similarities = cosine_similarity(user_item_matrix)

# Get recommendations for a target user
def recommend_items(user_id, user_similarities, item_data):
    # ... (code to identify similar users and recommend items based on their interactions)

# Example usage
```

```
recommendations                              =
recommend_items(target_user_id, user_similarities,
item_data)
print(f"Recommendations for user {target_user_id}:
{recommendations}")
```
Use code with caution.

content_copy

6. Beyond the Basics: Exploration and Refinement

Building a simple recommender system is a great starting point. As you venture further, you can explore more sophisticated techniques:

Matrix Factorization: A dimensionality reduction technique that can capture latent factors underlying user-item interactions.

Incorporating Additional Data: Include user demographics, implicit feedback (browsing history), or time-based factors for more personalized recommendations.

Evaluation Metrics: Metrics like precision-recall curves or recommendation accuracy can help assess your recommender system's effectiveness.

By understanding these core concepts, you'll be well-equipped to build basic recommender systems and delve deeper into the fascinating world of recommendation algorithms. Remember, the key is to leverage data effectively to create personalized recommendations that keep your users engaged.

10.1. Using collaborative filtering to recommend items

In the realm of recommender systems, collaborative filtering (CF) is a powerful technique that personalizes recommendations based on the wisdom of the crowds. Imagine you walk into a bookstore – CF is like a helpful clerk who suggests books similar to what others with similar tastes have enjoyed. Let's delve into how CF works:

1. The Core Idea: Learning from Like-Minded Users

Collaborative filtering makes the assumption that users with similar past preferences are likely to have similar future preferences. Here's the workflow:

User-Item Matrix: The foundation of CF is a user-item matrix. This matrix represents user interactions with items. Rows represent users, columns represent items, and each cell contains a value indicating the user's interaction with an item (e.g., rating, purchase history). Often, this matrix is sparse, with many empty cells due to users not having interacted with every item.

Similarity Measures: The next step is to quantify the similarity between users. Common similarity metrics include cosine similarity and Pearson correlation coefficient. These metrics assess how closely two users' tastes align based on their interaction patterns in the user-item matrix.

Recommendation Generation: For a target user, the system identifies the most similar users based on the calculated similarities. Then, it recommends items that these similar users have interacted with but the target user hasn't. The assumption is that the target user is likely to enjoy these items as well, since they share similar tastes with the users who liked them.

2. Advantages of Collaborative Filtering

Effective for Sparse Data: CF can be particularly useful when dealing with sparse data, where users haven't interacted with many items. By leveraging the preferences of similar users, it can still generate meaningful recommendations.

Captures User Preferences Beyond Item Features: Unlike content-based filtering which focuses on item features, CF goes beyond the surface and captures the complex and nuanced preferences of users.

3. Different Flavors of Collaborative Filtering

User-Based CF: This approach focuses on finding similar users to the target user and recommending items they have interacted with. As mentioned earlier, this is effective for sparse data but can become computationally expensive with a large user base.

Item-Based CF: This approach focuses on finding items similar to the items the target user has interacted with and recommending those similar items. This can be more scalable for large datasets but might struggle with new or unseen items (cold start problem).

Matrix Factorization: This advanced technique decomposes the user-item matrix into lower-dimensional matrices, capturing latent factors that underlie user-item interactions. This can address sparsity and scalability challenges.

4. Example: Movie Recommendations with User-Based CF

Imagine a movie recommender system. Here's a simplified example:

* User A likes movies 'The Godfather' and 'The Shawshank Redemption' (both crime dramas).
* User B likes 'The Godfather' and 'Casablanca' (crime drama and classic).
* User C likes 'The Shawshank Redemption' and 'The Lord of the Rings' (drama and fantasy).
Based on user similarities, User A might be recommended 'Casablanca' (similar taste to User B)

and User C might be recommended 'The Lord of the Rings' (similar taste to User A).

5. Beyond the Basics: Real-World Applications

Collaborative filtering is a cornerstone of recommender systems used in various applications:

E-commerce: Recommending products based on purchase history of similar customers.
Streaming Services: Recommending movies or music based on viewing/listening habits of similar users.

Social Media: Suggesting friends or content based on user interactions and connections.

By leveraging collaborative filtering, you can create recommender systems that unlock the power of user preferences, leading to more engaging and personalized user experiences. As you explore further, delve into the different CF techniques and explore how they can be applied to real-world recommender system problems.

Chapter 11

Creating a Chatbot with Natural Language Processing (NLP)

In today's digital world, chatbots are ubiquitous, acting as virtual assistants, answering customer queries, or guiding users through online experiences. But what brings these chatbots to life? Natural Language Processing (NLP) is the magic ingredient that enables them to understand and respond to human language. Here's a roadmap to navigate the creation of an NLP-powered chatbot:

1. Define Your Chatbot's Purpose: The Foundation for Conversation

Identify the Need: What problem will your chatbot solve? Will it answer customer service questions, schedule appointments, or provide product information?

Target Audience: Who will your chatbot interact with? Understanding their needs, language style, and expectations is crucial for designing effective conversations.

2. Building the Core Engine: Understanding and Responding

Natural Language Understanding (NLU): This is the crux of NLP. Your chatbot needs to interpret the user's intent (what they want to achieve) and extract meaning from their message. Techniques like intent recognition and entity extraction are used to achieve this.

Intent Recognition: Classifies the user's message into predefined categories (intents) like "order food," "check order status," or "cancel order."

Entity Extraction: Identifies specific details within the message, such as the food item being ordered or the order number.

Natural Language Generation (NLG): Once the user's intent is understood, it's time to craft a response. NLG techniques generate human-like text responses that fulfill the user's intent.

3. Tools and Technologies:

Programming Languages: Python is a popular choice due to its readability and extensive NLP libraries like NLTK, spaCy, and Rasa.
Chatbot Frameworks: Frameworks like Dialogflow, Rasa, and Microsoft Bot Framework provide pre-built functionalities for chatbot development, simplifying the process.

4. Training and Refinement: The Art of Conversation

Training Data: Providing your chatbot with a large corpus of training data (conversations, examples) is essential. This data helps the NLU component learn to interpret user messages and the NLG component generate natural-sounding responses.

Iterative Improvement: Continuously test your chatbot with real users and gather feedback. This allows you to identify areas for improvement, refine your training data, and fine-tune your NLP models for better performance.

5. Example: A Restaurant Recommendation Chatbot

Imagine a chatbot that helps users find restaurants. Here's a simplified breakdown:

* **NLU:** The chatbot understands the user's intent (find a restaurant) and extracts entities like cuisine (Italian) and location (downtown).

* **Action:** The chatbot searches for restaurants based on the extracted information.
* **NLG:** The chatbot generates a response suggesting restaurants that match the user's preferences.

6. Beyond the Basics: Advanced NLP Techniques

As you venture further, explore advanced NLP techniques to enhance your chatbot's capabilities:

Sentiment Analysis: Understand the emotional tone of the user's message to tailor responses accordingly.

Dialogue Management: Manage the flow of conversation, including handling clarification requests, following up on previous questions, and gracefully ending the interaction.

Machine Learning: Incorporate machine learning algorithms to personalize recommendations, improve intent recognition accuracy, and adapt to new user interactions over time.

By harnessing the power of NLP, you can build chatbots that engage in natural and informative conversations, ultimately providing a more satisfying user experience. Remember, the key is to focus on the user's needs, continuously refine your chatbot's abilities, and stay updated with the latest advancements in NLP technology.

11.1. Introduction to NLP concepts

Natural Language Processing (NLP) bridges the gap between computers and human language. It equips machines with the ability to understand, interpret, and generate human language, unlocking a world of possibilities for interaction and communication.

Here, we'll delve into some fundamental NLP concepts:

1. Tokenization: Breaking Down Text into Meaningful Units

Imagine you're building a puzzle. Tokenization is the first step, similar to separating the puzzle pieces. It involves segmenting a text message into smaller units called tokens. These tokens can be words, punctuation marks, or even phrases depending on the specific task.

2. Part-of-Speech (POS) Tagging: Labeling the Words

In a sentence, different words play different roles. POS tagging assigns a grammatical label (e.g., noun, verb, adjective) to each word in a sentence. This helps the computer understand the function of each word within the context of the sentence.

3. Named Entity Recognition (NER): Identifying Important Entities

Names of people, locations, organizations, and other relevant entities hold significant meaning in a text. NER aims to identify and classify these named entities within a sentence. Imagine recognizing the location (e.g., Paris) and person (e.g., John) in the sentence "John traveled to Paris."

4. Stemming and Lemmatization: Reducing Words to Their Base Form

The English language is full of variations of the same word (walk, walks, walked). Stemming and lemmatization aim to reduce words to their base form (stem or lemma) to improve efficiency and consistency in NLP tasks. Stemming uses a simple rule-based approach, while lemmatization considers the grammatical context to identify the correct base form.

5. Text Normalization: Cleaning Up the Text

Text data can be messy, containing typos, abbreviations, and informal language. Text normalization techniques address these issues by converting text to a more consistent format. This might involve correcting typos, expanding abbreviations, or converting text to lowercase for easier processing.

6. N-Grams: Capturing Word Sequences

NLP often deals with sequences of words. N-grams are a powerful concept that captures these sequences. An n-gram is a contiguous sequence of n words in a sentence. For instance, bigrams (2-grams) capture the relationship between pairs of words, while trigrams (3-grams) capture the relationship between three consecutive words.

7. Stop Words: Removing Common Uninformative Words

Not all words in a sentence contribute significantly to meaning. Stop words are common words like "the," "a," "an," or "is" that can be filtered out without affecting the core meaning of the text. This can improve processing efficiency and focus on the more informative content.

8. Word Embeddings: Representing Words as Vectors

Imagine representing words as points in a high-dimensional space. Word embeddings are a powerful technique that assigns a numerical vector to each word, where words with similar meanings have similar vectors. This allows NLP models to capture semantic relationships between words and perform tasks like word similarity or analogy detection.

These are just a few foundational concepts in NLP. As you delve deeper, you'll explore more advanced topics like sentiment analysis, machine translation, and dialogue systems, empowering you to build intelligent applications that interact with human language in increasingly sophisticated ways.

11.2. Building a basic chatbot

The world of chatbots is booming, and with a bit of know-how, you can build your own! Here's a roadmap to get you started creating a basic chatbot:

1. Define the Purpose and Scope: Charting the Course

What will your chatbot do? Will it answer FAQs, schedule appointments, or provide simple customer service? Clearly defining the purpose helps guide its development.

Who will it interact with? Understanding your target audience (their age group, technical proficiency) is crucial for designing suitable interactions.

2. Choosing the Tools: Bricks and Mortar for Your Bot

Programming Language: Python is a popular choice due to its readability and extensive NLP libraries like NLTK and spaCy.

Chatbot Frameworks (Optional): Simplify development with pre-built functionalities. Dialogflow, Rasa, and Microsoft Bot Framework are some options.

3. Core Functionality: Understanding and Responding

Intents: Define the different actions your chatbot can handle (e.g., "greet user," "answer question about product X").

Entities: Identify specific pieces of information users might provide (e.g., product name, location).
Natural Language Understanding (NLU): The brain of your chatbot. It uses techniques like pattern matching or machine learning to recognize user intent and extract entities from their messages.

4. Crafting Responses: The Art of Conversation

Define Responses: Create natural-sounding responses for each intent, potentially with variations to avoid repetitiveness.
Placeholders: Use placeholders like {name} to personalize responses by incorporating extracted

entities (e.g., "Hi {name}, how can I help you today?").

5. Putting It All Together: Coding the Chatbot

Write the code: Use your chosen language and libraries to implement the NLU functionalities, response selection, and conversation flow.
Test and Refine: Continuously test your chatbot with various user inputs and iterate on your code to improve its accuracy and responsiveness.
6. Example: A Simple FAQ Chatbot

Imagine a chatbot that answers frequently asked questions (FAQs) about a clothing store. Here's a simplified breakdown:

* **Intents:** greet, ask about product X, ask return policy, etc.
* **Entities:** product name (for questions about specific products).

* **NLU:** Matches user queries to predefined intents and extracts entities.

* **Responses:** The chatbot has pre-defined responses for each intent, potentially incorporating placeholders for entities.

7. Beyond the Basics: Adding Personality and Complexity

As you explore further, you can enhance your chatbot with:

Dialogue Management: Control the conversation flow, including handling clarification requests and following up on previous questions.

Machine Learning: Train your chatbot on real conversation data to improve NLU accuracy and personalize responses.

External APIs: Integrate with external APIs to provide more informative responses (e.g., weather information, product availability).

Building a basic chatbot is a great introduction to the exciting world of conversational AI. Remember, the key is to start simple, focus on a clear purpose, and continuously improve your chatbot's abilities through testing and refinement.

Chapter 12
Exploring Computer Vision with Image Classification

Computer vision is a fascinating field of artificial intelligence (AI) that equips machines with the ability to "see" and understand the visual world. Image classification, a fundamental task within computer vision, empowers computers to analyze images and categorize them into predefined classes. Let's delve into this captivating realm:

1. The Core Idea: Labeling Images with Intelligence

Imagine showing a child a picture and asking them if it's a cat or a dog. Image classification automates this process for computers. It involves training a model to analyze an image, recognize the objects or scenes within it, and assign the most appropriate label (cat, dog, etc.) from a set of predefined categories.

2. Applications of Image Classification:

Self-driving Cars: Classifying objects like pedestrians, traffic lights, and other vehicles is crucial for safe navigation.

Medical Diagnosis: Analyzing medical scans (X-rays, MRIs) to identify abnormalities or specific diseases.

Product Recognition: Classifying objects in images for tasks like content moderation or image search.

Satellite Image Analysis: Understanding land cover types (forests, cities) or identifying changes over time.

3. The Machine Learning Process:

Training Data: The foundation of image classification models is a large collection of labeled images. Each image is associated with a correct category label (e.g., cat, dog).

Feature Extraction: The model analyzes the training images and extracts features that differentiate between categories. These features could be edges, shapes, colors, or textures within the image.

Classification Algorithm: Common algorithms include K-Nearest Neighbors (KNN), Support Vector Machines (SVMs), and Convolutional Neural Networks (CNNs). The chosen algorithm learns from the features and training data to build a model that can classify new unseen images.

4. Convolutional Neural Networks (CNNs): The Powerhouse of Image Classification

CNNs are a special type of neural network architecture specifically designed for image data. They are particularly adept at capturing spatial relationships between pixels within an image, a crucial aspect for accurate classification. CNNs consist of multiple layers that progressively extract higher-level features from the image, ultimately leading to the classification output.

5. Building an Image Classifier with Python Libraries

Libraries like TensorFlow and PyTorch provide powerful tools for building and training image classification models in Python. Here's a glimpse of the process:

Python
```
# Import libraries and load data (images and labels)
from tensorflow.keras.datasets import cifar10
(train_images,      train_labels),      (test_images,
test_labels) = cifar10.load_data()

# Preprocess data (normalize pixel values)
train_images = train_images.astype('float32') / 255.0
test_images = test_images.astype('float32') / 255.0
```

```python
# Define the CNN model architecture
from tensorflow.keras.models import Sequential
from tensorflow.keras.layers import Conv2D,
MaxPooling2D, Flatten, Dense

model = Sequential()
#   ...   (add   convolutional,   pooling,   and
fully-connected layers)

# Compile and train the model
model.compile(optimizer='adam',
loss='sparse_categorical_crossentropy',
metrics=['accuracy'])
model.fit(train_images, train_labels, epochs=5)

# Evaluate the model on test data
test_loss, test_acc = model.evaluate(test_images,
test_labels)
print("Test accuracy:", test_acc)
```
Use code with caution.
content_copy

6. Beyond the Basics: Exploring Advanced Techniques

As you venture further into the realm of computer vision, you'll delve into:

Transfer Learning: Leverage pre-trained models on large datasets (like ImageNet) to improve the performance of your image classifier.

Object Detection: Not only classify objects but also identify their location within the image (bounding boxes).

Image Segmentation: Classify every pixel in the image, providing a more detailed understanding of the image content.

By unlocking the power of image classification, you'll be well on your way to exploring the exciting world of computer vision and its potential applications in various domains. Remember, the key is to start with a solid foundation in image classification and then gradually progress towards more complex computer vision tasks.

12.1. Loading and processing images

In computer vision, images are the gateway to a world of visual information. But before working their magic, these images need to be loaded, processed, and transformed into a format suitable for analysis by computer vision algorithms. Here's a roadmap to navigate this crucial first step:

1. Loading Images: Bridging the Gap Between Files and Data

Libraries: Popular libraries like OpenCV (Open Source Computer Vision Library) and Pillow (Friendly Fork of PIL Fork of Python Imaging Library) offer functions to read images from various file formats (JPEG, PNG, BMP) into memory.

Common Functions: cv2.imread (OpenCV) and Image.open (Pillow) are frequently used functions to load images. They take the image file path as input and return an image object that can be manipulated further.

2. Exploring Image Properties: Understanding the Data

Image Data Type: Loaded images are typically represented as NumPy arrays, where each element corresponds to a pixel value. The data type of these elements (uint8 for color images, float64 for grayscale) determines how intensity values are stored.

Shape and Channels: The image shape is a tuple indicating the number of rows, columns, and channels. For color images, there are typically 3 channels (RGB), while grayscale images have 1 channel.

3. Grayscale Conversion: Simplifying the Color World

Color to Grayscale: Sometimes, color information is irrelevant or may even add complexity to the analysis. Conversion to grayscale reduces an image to a single channel representing intensity levels at each pixel.

Conversion Techniques: OpenCV and Pillow provide functions like cv2.cvtColor and Image.convert to achieve grayscale conversion.

4. Resizing Images: Scaling to Fit

Resizing Needs: Image size can significantly impact processing time and memory requirements. Resizing images to a standard size ensures consistency and can improve efficiency.

Resizing Techniques: Libraries offer functions like cv2.resize and Image.resize to modify image dimensions. Different interpolation methods (e.g., nearest neighbor, bilinear) can be used to control how pixels are resampled during resizing.

5. Normalization: Putting Pixels on the Same Page

Normalization Importance: The range of pixel values in an image can vary depending on the acquisition process. Normalization scales pixel intensities to a common range (often 0 to 1 or -1 to 1) to facilitate better performance in computer vision algorithms.

Normalization Techniques: Common approaches include subtracting the mean pixel value and dividing by the standard deviation across the entire image or each channel (for color images).

6. Data Augmentation: Artificially Expanding Your Dataset

Overfitting Prevention: Limited training data can lead to overfitting, where a model performs well on the training data but poorly on unseen data. Data augmentation artificially creates new variations of existing images to enrich the training dataset and improve generalization.

Augmentation Techniques: Random flips, rotations, crops, brightness adjustments, and noise addition are some common data augmentation techniques.

7. Beyond the Basics: Advanced Preprocessing Techniques

As you delve deeper, explore more specialized preprocessing techniques:

Noise Reduction: Techniques to remove unwanted noise patterns from images.

Color Correction: Adjusting color balance or correcting for lighting variations.

Image Segmentation: Dividing the image into meaningful regions for object-level analysis.

By effectively loading and processing images, you'll prepare them for computer vision algorithms, unlocking their potential to extract meaningful information from the visual world. Remember, the choice of preprocessing techniques depends on the specific task and image characteristics.

12.2. Building a model to classify images

In the realm of computer vision, image classification empowers computers to categorize images into predefined classes. But how do we translate pixels into meaningful labels? Here's a roadmap to building a model for image recognition:

1. Choosing the Right Tool for the Job

Machine Learning Algorithms: Traditional machine learning algorithms like Support Vector Machines (SVMs) or K-Nearest Neighbors (KNN) can be used for image classification, but their performance often lags behind deep learning approaches.

Deep Learning with Convolutional Neural Networks (CNNs): The current state-of-the-art for image classification. CNNs are specifically designed to excel at extracting features from image data and achieve superior classification accuracy.

2. Deep Dive into Convolutional Neural Networks (CNNs)

Core Building Blocks: CNNs consist of convolutional layers, pooling layers, and fully-connected layers. Convolutional layers learn filters that detect specific features within the image (edges, shapes, colors). Pooling layers reduce the dimensionality of the data while preserving important features. Fully-connected layers at the end of the network perform the final classification.

Network Architectures: Popular architectures like VGG16, ResNet, and Inception have been pre-trained on massive datasets (ImageNet) and can be fine-tuned for your specific classification task.

3. Building Your CNN with Libraries like TensorFlow or PyTorch

These libraries provide user-friendly tools to define, train, and evaluate your CNN model. Here's a simplified example using TensorFlow:

```Python
from tensorflow.keras.models import Sequential
from tensorflow.keras.layers import Conv2D, MaxPooling2D, Flatten, Dense

# Define the CNN architecture
model = Sequential()
model.add(Conv2D(32, (3, 3), activation='relu', input_shape=(img_height, img_width, 3)))
model.add(MaxPooling2D((2, 2)))
# ... (add more convolutional and pooling layers)
model.add(Flatten())
model.add(Dense(128, activation='relu'))
```

```
model.add(Dense(num_classes,
activation='softmax'))

# Compile the model (specifying optimizer, loss
function, metrics)
model.compile(optimizer='adam',
loss='sparse_categorical_crossentropy',
metrics=['accuracy'])
```
Use code with caution.

content_copy

4. Training Your Model: Feeding it Knowledge

Training Data: The cornerstone of model performance. Your data should consist of a collection of labeled images, where each image belongs to a specific class. The larger and more diverse the dataset, the better the model will generalize to unseen images.

Training Process: The model iterates through the training data, adjusting its internal parameters (weights and biases) to minimize the classification error on the training images. This process, called gradient descent, is guided by an optimizer like Adam.

5. Evaluating Model Performance: Assessing Strengths and Weaknesses

Validation Set: A separate set of labeled images used to monitor the model's performance during training and prevent overfitting. Overfitting occurs when the model memorizes the training data but fails to generalize well to unseen images.

Metrics: Track metrics like accuracy (percentage of images correctly classified) and loss (a measure of classification error) to gauge the model's effectiveness.

6. Fine-Tuning Pre-trained Models: Leveraging the Power of Pre-training

Transfer Learning: Pre-trained models on large datasets (like ImageNet) have already learned powerful features for image recognition. You can leverage this knowledge by fine-tuning these models on your specific dataset, often achieving excellent results without requiring massive amounts of training data from scratch.

7. Beyond the Basics: Advanced Architectures and Techniques

As you explore further, delve into:

Regularization Techniques: Prevent overfitting with techniques like dropout or L1/L2 regularization.

Data Augmentation: Artificially expand your dataset to improve modelgeneralizability (covered in previous section on loading and processing images).

Ensemble Learning: Combine multiple CNN models to potentially achieve better performance than a single model.

Building a model for image classification opens doors to exciting computer vision applications. Remember, the key is to understand the core concepts, choose the right tools and techniques, and continuously evaluate and refine your model for optimal performance.

Part 5: Next Steps and Resources

Chapter 13

Deep Learning and Advanced AI Techniques

Deep learning, a subfield of artificial intelligence (AI), has revolutionized various tasks from image recognition to natural language processing. By mimicking the structure and function of the human brain, deep learning models achieve remarkable results on complex problems. Here, we'll explore the core principles and delve into some advanced AI techniques:

1. Deep Learning Fundamentals: Artificial Neural Networks

The foundation of deep learning lies in artificial neural networks. These are interconnected layers of artificial neurons, inspired by biological neurons. Each neuron performs a simple computation on its inputs and transmits the output to connected neurons in the next layer. Deep learning models typically have many layers, enabling them to learn complex patterns from data.

Activation Functions: These functions introduce non-linearity into the network, allowing it to learn more intricate relationships between input features and the desired output. Popular activation functions include ReLU (Rectified Linear Unit) and sigmoid.

2. Training Deep Learning Models: Gradient Descent

Deep learning models learn by iteratively adjusting their internal parameters (weights and biases) to minimize a loss function. This loss function quantifies the difference between the model's predictions and the actual targets. Gradient descent is an optimization algorithm that guides this adjustment process. It calculates the gradients (slopes) of the loss function with respect to the weights and biases, and then updates them in a direction that minimizes the loss.

3. Popular Deep Learning Architectures

Convolutional Neural Networks (CNNs): Excel at image recognition tasks. CNNs use convolutional layers with learnable filters to extract features from images. These features are then processed by pooling layers and fully-connected layers for classification or regression tasks.

Recurrent Neural Networks (RNNs): Designed to handle sequential data like text or time series. RNNs process information sequentially, allowing them to capture dependencies between elements in a sequence. Long Short-Term Memory (LSTM) and Gated Recurrent Unit (GRU) are special types of RNNs that can learn long-term dependencies.

4. Advanced AI Techniques: Pushing the Boundaries

As you venture further into the realm of AI, you'll encounter even more sophisticated techniques:

Generative Adversarial Networks (GANs): Two neural networks compete with each other. One (generator) tries to create realistic data (e.g., images, text), while the other (discriminator) tries to distinguish real data from the generated data. This adversarial process leads to the generation of increasingly realistic data.

Reinforcement Learning: Trains AI agents through trial and error in an interactive environment. The agent receives rewards for desired actions and penalties for undesired actions, allowing it to learn optimal strategies over time. This is a powerful approach for training agents for complex decision-making tasks in games or robotics.

Attention Mechanisms: A technique used in deep learning models to focus on specific parts of the input data that are most relevant for the task at hand. This is particularly useful in tasks like machine translation or question answering, where understanding the context is crucial.

5. Deep Learning Frameworks: Tools for Building AI Systems

Developing deep learning models from scratch can be cumbersome. Thankfully, there are powerful frameworks available to simplify the process:

TensorFlow: An open-source framework developed by Google, offering a flexible and powerful platform for building and deploying deep learning models.

PyTorch: Another open-source framework, known for its ease of use and dynamic computational graph.

Keras: A high-level API that can be used on top of TensorFlow or other frameworks, providing a simpler interface for building neural networks.

6. The Future of Deep Learning and AI

Deep learning and advanced AI techniques continue to evolve rapidly, creating new possibilities across various domains. As research progresses, we can expect to see further advancements in:

Explainable AI (XAI): Making AI models more transparent and interpretable, allowing us to understand how they arrive at their decisions.

Responsible AI: Developing AI systems that are fair, unbiased, and aligned with human values.

Neuromorphic Computing: Designing hardware specifically inspired by the brain to accelerate deep learning computations.

By understanding the core principles of deep learning and exploring advanced AI techniques, you'll be well-equipped to contribute to the exciting future of artificial intelligence. Remember, the responsible development and application of AI are crucial aspects of this ever-evolving field.

13.1. Introduction to deep learning and neural networks

Deep learning, a branch of artificial intelligence (AI), has become a game-changer across various fields. By mimicking the structure and function of the human brain, deep learning models are capable of remarkable feats in areas like image recognition, natural language processing, and more. Let's embark on a journey to understand the fundamentals of deep learning and its core component – neural networks.

1. Artificial Neural Networks: Inspired by the Brain

Imagine a web of interconnected nodes, loosely inspired by biological neurons. This is the essence of an artificial neural network. These networks consist of layers – input layers, hidden layers, and an output layer. Information flows from the input layer, through hidden layers (where complex computations occur), and finally to the output layer, which delivers the network's prediction or decision.

Neurons: The building blocks, processing information and transmitting signals to other neurons. Each neuron applies a mathematical function (activation function) to its inputs to determine its output.

Connections: The pathways between neurons, carrying signals with varying strengths (weights). These weights are crucial for learning, as the network adjusts them to improve its performance.

2. Deep Learning: The Power of Many Layers

While traditional neural networks might have few layers, deep learning models have many layers stacked on top of each other. This allows them to learn increasingly intricate patterns within data. Imagine recognizing a cat in an image – the first layers might detect edges and shapes, while later layers learn to combine these features to identify the complete cat.

3. Training Deep Learning Models: Learning from Experience

Deep learning models don't magically know how to perform tasks. They require training on vast amounts of data. Here's a simplified view of the training process:

Data Preparation: The data is fed into the network, with each data point having an expected output (e.g., an image of a cat labeled as "cat").
Forward Pass: Information travels through the network, generating an initial prediction (e.g., the network might guess "dog").

Error Calculation: The difference between the predicted output and the actual output is calculated (the error).

Backward Pass: The error is propagated back through the network, adjusting the weights of the connections to minimize the error for future predictions.

Optimization: This process (forward pass, error calculation, backward pass) is repeated iteratively, with the network gradually improving its accuracy.

4. Popular Deep Learning Architectures

Deep learning boasts a diverse toolbox of architectures, each suited for specific tasks:

Convolutional Neural Networks (CNNs): Champions of image recognition. CNNs use convolutional layers with learnable filters to identify edges, shapes, and textures within images, ultimately leading to object classification.

Recurrent Neural Networks (RNNs): Designed for sequential data like text or speech. RNNs process information sequentially, allowing them to capture the relationships between words in a sentence or sounds in speech.

5. Beyond the Basics: Exploring Advanced Concepts

As you delve deeper, the world of deep learning offers a treasure trove of advanced topics:

Activation Functions: These functions introduce non-linearity into the network, enabling it to learn complex relationships between data points.

Gradient Descent: An optimization algorithm that guides the training process by adjusting the weights of the connections within the network.

Loss Functions: Measure how well the model's predictions deviate from the actual targets.

6. Deep Learning Frameworks: Building Blocks for AI Systems

Developing deep learning models from scratch can be daunting. Thankfully, frameworks like TensorFlow, PyTorch, and Keras provide user-friendly tools to simplify the process. These frameworks offer pre-built functions and components, allowing you to focus on the core concepts and applications.

By understanding the fundamentals of deep learning and neural networks, you'll be well on your way to unlocking the potential of this revolutionary technology. Remember, deep learning is a rapidly evolving field, so stay curious and keep exploring the exciting possibilities it holds!

13.2. Resources for further exploration

The world of deep learning is vast and ever-expanding. To empower your exploration, here's a treasure map of resources to guide you on your path:

1. Online Courses and Tutorials:

Platforms:

Coursera: Offers well-structured courses from top universities and companies, like "Deep Learning Specialization" by Andrew Ng. (https://www.coursera.org/specializations/deep-lear ning)
Udacity: Provides project-oriented Nanodegrees, like "Intro to Deep Learning" which equips you with practical skills. ([invalid URL removed])
fast.ai: Practical deep learning courses with a focus on simplicity and getting you started quickly. (https://www.fast.ai/)

YouTube Channels:

DeepLearning.TV: A comprehensive channel with tutorials, lectures, and discussions by experts. ([invalid URL removed])

3Blue1Brown: Makes complex concepts like neural networks engaging and visually intuitive. ([invalid URL removed])

2. Books:

"Deep Learning" by Ian Goodfellow, Yoshua Bengio, and Aaron Courville: A comprehensive reference book, delving into the theory and algorithms behind deep learning. (https://www.deeplearningbook.org/)
"Hands-On Machine Learning with Scikit-Learn, Keras & TensorFlow" by Aurélien Géron: A practical guide applying deep learning techniques using popular libraries. ([invalid URL removed])
"

The Hundred-Page Machine Learning Book" by

Andriy Burkov: A concise introduction to machine learning concepts, including deep learning fundamentals. ([invalid URL removed])

3. Documentations and Blogs:

TensorFlow: Extensive documentation, tutorials, and guides for using TensorFlow, a popular deep learning framework. (https://www.tensorflow.org/tutorials)

PyTorch: Clear documentation and tutorials for PyTorch, another powerful deep learning framework. (https://pytorch.org/tutorials/)

Machine Learning Mastery: A blog by Michael Nielsen, covering a wide range of machine learning topics, including deep learning. (https://machinelearningmastery.com/deep-learning/)

4. Online Communities and Forums:

Reddit's r/MachineLearning: A large and active community for discussions, Q&A, and sharing deep

learning   resources.
(https://www.reddit.com/r/MachineLearning/)
Kaggle: A platform for data science competitions and discussions. Participate in challenges to apply your deep learning skills in a practical setting. (https://www.kaggle.com/)

OpenAI Blog: Stay updated on the latest advancements in deep learning research from a leading AI research lab. (https://openai.com/blog/)

Remember, consistent practice is key to mastering deep learning. Explore these resources, experiment with code, and actively engage with the online communities to solidify your understanding and propel your deep learning journey.

www.ingramcontent.com/pod-product-compliance
Lightning Source LLC
La Vergne TN
LVHW051330050326
832903LV00031B/3460